WEST ORANGE LIBRARY
46 MT. PLEASANT AVENUE
WEST ORANGE, NJ 07052
(201) 736-0198

D1294694

MUSHROOMS

MUSHROOMS

WEST ORANGE LIBRARY
46 MT. PLEASANT AVENUE
WEST ORANGE, NJ 07052
(201) 736-0198

PETER MURRAY

THE CHILD'S WORLD®

You see something in the grass, a white bump. At first, you don't know what it is. Is it a golf ball? A scrap of paper? A frosted cupcake? Whatever it is, it wasn't there yesterday! You take a closer look.

Oh. It's only a mushroom. You've seen lots of mushrooms before. Maybe you've even eaten the ones sold at the grocery store. You start to walk away, but then you start to wonder.

What is a mushroom, anyway? And where did this one come from?

In ancient times, people noticed that mushrooms usually appeared after a rainstorm. Some people thought they were caused by lightning. Stories were told of fairies using them as umbrellas, or of toads using them for stools. Even today we call circles of mushrooms *fairy rings,* and we still call some mushrooms *toadstools.*

Lightning, fairies, and toads don't really cause mushrooms to grow. The origin of mushrooms lies deep underground. The mushroom you see is only a small part of a much bigger story.

Green plants such as trees and grasses make their own food from soil, sunlight, and water. But mushrooms are members of a plant kingdom called the *fungi*. Unlike the green plants, fungi must take their food from other plants.

Have you ever looked under a pile of old leaves, or peeled the bark off a rotting log? You might have seen a layer of white, cottony material growing there. The white material is called *mycelium.* Mycelium is the body of a fungus. It absorbs moisture and food from the surrounding plant material. Without mycelium, there would be no mushrooms.

When it rains, the underground mycelium absorbs water quickly. Wet weather is the fungus's opportunity to reproduce. Small, solid bumps appear on the cottony threads. The bumps enlarge and push up out of the ground, taking on the familiar umbrella shape of the mushroom.

The mushroom you see is actually the *fruit* of the fungus plant.

As the mushroom grows larger, its cap expands and reveals thin blades of tissue radiating out from the stem. These are called the *gills*, and they are covered with millions of *spores*. Spores, like the seeds of an apple, are the fungus's way of reproducing itself.

Spores are so light and tiny you need a microscope to see one. They are carried away by the wind, or by insects, or by passing animals. Of the millions of spores produced by a single mushroom, only a few will land in a place where they can grow into a new network of mycelium.

When millions of spores are clustered together, they look like dust. Try this experiment: Place the cap of a mushroom on a piece of paper and cover it with a bowl. A few hours later, you will have a *spore print* on the paper. Scientists use the color of the spore print to help them identify different mushrooms.

Some mushrooms do not have gills. Mushrooms in the *boletus* family, for example, have tiny tubes under their caps.

Puffballs are leathery sacs filled with dark brown spores. When you squeeze a ripe puffball, a cloud of spores puffs out. The giant puffball, one of the largest of all mushrooms, can grow to more than four feet across!

The *morel* mushroom produces spores all over the wrinkled surface of its cap. Every spring, mushroom hunters take to the woods in search of the hard-to-find morel, a prized edible mushroom.

The mushrooms found in most grocery stores are related to the common meadow mushroom. People grow these mushrooms in caves or in special buildings where the temperature and humidity are tightly controlled. Under these ideal conditions, mushrooms can be harvested every day.

Today, many unusual mushroom varieties are also being farmed. The *shitake* mushroom from Japan is grown on logs. The *oyster* mushroom, which grows wild on trees, is now cultivated on beds of straw. Even the scarce morel mushroom may one day become a cultivated crop.

Human beings have been eating mushrooms for millions of years. But not all mushrooms are good to eat. Of the thousands of known mushroom species, more than half are bad-tasting, unappetizing, or poisonous. The beautiful *death angel* mushroom is so deadly poisonous that a single bite might send you to the hospital. Many careless mushroom hunters have gotten sick or died from eating the wrong fungus.

Unfortunately, there is no easy test that will tell you if a mushroom is poisonous. The best rule is, look but don't taste! Only an experienced, knowledgeable mushroom hunter knows how to tell the good from the bad.

Some mushrooms, such as the meadow mushroom, rely on dead plant matter for food. They are called *saprophytes*. Other mushrooms, called *parasites*, take their nourishment from living plants. Parasitic mushrooms can cause great harm to the plants upon which they feed. Many tree diseases are caused by mushrooms like the *honeycap*. The honeycap is a small honey-colored mushroom that can send its mycelium deep into the living tissue of the tree trunk. Some parasitic fungi attack insects, sending tiny mushrooms up from the insect's dead body. Even mushrooms themselves are not immune from other parasitic mushrooms!

Scientists have discovered more than five thousand species of mushrooms, each with its own size, shape, color, and growing habits. Like animals and green plants, mushrooms have an important role in the cycle of nature. Tiny threads of mycelium help break down dead plants, returning nutrients to the soil so that other plants can grow. Even the parasitic mushrooms help the environment grow stronger by destroying weak and diseased trees. Mushrooms also provide food for both people and animals. Even squirrels enjoy a bite of mushroom now and then!

INDEX

Photo Research
Kristee Flynn

Photo Credits
COMSTOCK/Art Gingert: cover
COMSTOCK/Gwen Fidler: 2
Wyman P. Meinzer: 4
Robert & Linda Mitchell: 7, 8, 11, 13, 14, 21
Joy Spurr: 17, 22, 27, 31
PHOTO RESEARCHERS, INC./Carleton Ray: 18
PHOTO RESEARCHERS, INC./Rod Planck: 24
PHOTO RESEARCHERS, INC./Scott Camazine: 28

Text Copyright © 1996 by The Child's World®, Inc.
All rights reserved. No part of this book may be
reproduced or utilized in any form or by any means
without written permission from the publisher.
Printed in the United States of America.

Library of Congress Cataloging-in-Publication Data
Murray, Peter, 1952 Sept. 29-
Mushrooms / by Peter Murray.
p. cm.
Includes Index.
ISBN 1-56766-193-9

1. Mushrooms--Juvenile literature. [1. Mushrooms.] I. Title.
QK617.M79   1995   95-907
589.2'22--dc20